This Country Life

Also by Eliza Rusk

This Country Life - Old Houses

To Nancy,
My gracious friend!
Much love,
Eliza Rusk *

* aka Heather Beach

This Country Life

ANIMAL STORIES

Eliza Rusk

With Illustrations by Susan Jackson

ISBN: 1542347408
ISBN 13: 9781542347402

for Nora and Pat
Annabelle and Cameron
Araya, Aleecea and Auburn

Animal lovers all!

"Some people talk to animals. Not many listen though. That's the problem."

- A.A. MILNE

Introduction

OH, WHAT THESE ANIMALS DO for our souls! For many of us, a life devoid of furry or feathered friends is inconceivable. In writing, and reliving, the stories in this book I have shed more tears than I thought possible. The memory of each creature has a permanent place in my heart. Note - I do not say that I "owned" these animals. We don't own *them* - It's more accurate to say that, during their brief lives, they own us.

When humans pass from the earth, a funeral or wake afford family members and friends a chance to remember and share stories about the loved one, to celebrate a life well-lived. The loss of an *animal* is often felt by very few. The world demands a quick recovery. A year after losing a parakeet or pet guinea pig, no one calls into work sick, citing their lingering grief or bursts into tears at the mention of the animal's name. Friends encourage us to "get a puppy" or to "think of the mess she made. No more cage to clean!"

Yet, each precious animal life is worthy of celebration. As I embark on my journey of remembrance…

Their faces, and limps and yelps and funny ways come back. They re-inhabit their mats and stalls. A dog who hunted frogs, and a yellow cat hanging out with a flock of sheep. The chicken and goat who, rejected by peers, shared a stall; and a gimpy, spotted goat who thought she was a horse.

I offer up these tales as a collection of eulogies for the animals I have loved and who have owned me.

Acknowledgements

SO MANY THANKS TO MY husband Bill and to our wonderful creative family. To Jenny for years of fun with horses, dogs and chickens and to animal lovers Chrissi (cats), Susie, Barb T. (chickens) and Judy (those pesky pigs!) Laura for loyal friendship, Sarah J. for good times in cold barns. To Katie for your company on the writer's path.

Lastly, my love and thanks to the Garfield Gang - world's best neighbors for enduring wild corgis and <u>always</u>, livestock on the loose!

Contents

Photographs

CHAPTER 1

Why Animals?

I DON'T CLAIM TO BE an authority on any species of animal. Horse people know more than I ever will. Likewise those who tend goats, sheep or cattle on a large scale could teach me a thing or two. However, spending time in the company of my animals has, I believe, provided an insight into other members of each breed. While not an expert, I am an animal <u>lover.</u>

Many friends interpret my compulsion to adopt, feed, chase and care for critters as a type of madness. No argument there. Now in the seventh decade of life, I reflect on this irrational drive to nurture and to be surrounded by birds and beasts. Why do we animal lovers do what we do? The answer is different for each stage of life:

For children, having a pet provides emotional support and unconditional love. Kids enjoy the chance to nurture another being and the companionship that cuddly friends provide. In research with preschool children, psychologists at Oregon State University found that teaching children to care for a puppy enhanced social skills:

"It made the children more cooperative and sharing," said Dr. Sue Doescher, a psychologist involved in the study. "Having a pet improves children's role-taking skills because they have to put themselves in the pet's position and try to feel how the pet feels. And that transfers to how other kids feel." [1]

For young adults, adopting a pet may be an attempt to fill a void, to replace the interaction with family and school friends we enjoyed in childhood. Before you know it, you're busy feeding, walking, grooming and cleaning up after your pet. Loneliness and home-sickness are forgotten. Naturally, you miss your brother or sister. But there's this: pets will never steal your clothes or boyfriends!

Newlywed couples may adopt a pet as a lifestyle experiment, a dress rehearsal for dealing with children. (Small wonder then, that we raise the kids we do.) Keeping dogs locked in crates for hours with a desiccated rawhide chew or watching over pigs as they wallow in their own filth: it's all good experience. And, when you *do* have

---

[1] http://www.nytimes.com/1990/01/11/us/health-children-and-their-pets-unexpected-psychological-benefits.html

children, it helps lend weight to the words *"Your room looks like a pigsty!"* when you actually know whereof you speak.

As parents, pets act as companions for our children, they teach responsibility. All those guinea pigs, gerbils, goldfish, ponies! Yet animals can help us stay connected to our kids. Without Saturday horse shows there's little chance my 15 year old and I would be seeking each other's company at six in the morning, driving for hours and spending the day hanging out with each other.

At some point, when our teenagers begin dating and then head off to college, it's animals that fill the void, once again. Not to mention the animals left behind *by* those teens. Many of my friends are raising grand dogs and cats for their children, whose lifestyles won't accommodate them.

In retirement, keeping animals provides the daily structure some of us require: feeding, watering and cleaning up the barn. Our creatures reward us with their affection. We argue that it's the grandchildren who need a pony to ride, a dog to walk and eggs to collect. Who are we kidding?

When life has dealt its blows and we've survived the pain of love and loss, four-footed friends come to our aid and help us heal.

They give life meaning. We rescue an orphan or stray animal, and they rescue us.

Large or small, indoors or out, animals enhance the quality of our existence at every stage of our lives.

CHAPTER 2

Sheep

It was a college Book Sale. The musty old volume was wedged under a pile of others. I pried it out, turned it over and read the spine: *Sheep Production*. Inside: *First Edition, 1927*. Perfect. I had just assembled my first flock of sheep. This book sale find was an answer to prayer. It cost one dollar.

I ran my hand across its coarse fabric binding, picturing the former owner, a farmer, gaining an encyclopedic knowledge of sheep husbandry by poring over this very manual. No doubt he'd lived to a ripe old age, dining on lamb stew, before donating the book to his alma mater for its annual sale. I added it to my cache and checked out.

After tending to my four ewes that evening, I grabbed the *sheep production bible* and settled into a comfy chair to bone up on the subject. Tucked into Chapter One was a faded scrap of paper - a hand-written memo. "It's a bit of sage advice," I thought, " from one shepherd to another. Addressed to the book's new owner." The notion made me giddy. *We're kindred spirits we sheep people. Living the simple life and passing on what we've learned.* I read out loud:

MEMO FROM THE DESK OF :
Lammot Dupont Copeland - President, Dupont Corporation
TO: Mr. Elwyn Evans - President, Wilmington Trust Co."
Elwyn-
May your sheep live longer than mine did. Do NOT return!
- Mots

The author of the memo was indeed Lammot Dupont Copeland of the prominent Delaware Dupont family. A powerful character in the nineteen sixties, he was a dominant figure at the highest levels of international business and politics, involved in chemical and defense contracts - featured on the cover of Time Magazine!

Copeland's estates in Delaware and on Maryland's Eastern Shore were models of best farm practices and conservation, his ancestors famous for breeding prize livestock.

"Oh dear," I thought. "If this gentleman farmer with *his* resources and intellect couldn't keep a few sheep alive, what hope was there for me?"

Over the next three decades I would come to appreciate the peculiar challenges that sheep rearing presents.

Sheep are misunderstood. Judging by their lack of individual personality and common sense, it's easy to assume they're brainless. Not so. It takes true genius for an animal to devise so many clever ways to kill itself or land in harm's way.

One can take every precaution with sheep. Do everything right. And still...

If there's a toxic plant they'll find it. A savage predator? They'll surrender. I've never, EVER, met a sheep who had the slightest interest in survival. "Dear sheep," you'll tell them. "I'm doing this for your own good." Don't expect them to care.

One problem is that sheep are herd (i.e. flock) bound, prone to follow the back end of the sheep in front. Unfortunately, their leaders are born followers also. Case in point:

One winter, during a late night ice storm, I was helping my friend coax her flock uphill to the safety of the barn. A thick, frozen crust had formed over the knee-deep snow. The sheep couldn't get a foothold - they were slipping all over! We had made great headway, by baby-steps, breaking a trail ahead of them. Finally, at the top of the hill, a few feet from shelter (*so* close to home!) the lead ewe came to a dead halt, turned and, seeing the rest of her girlfriends behind her, headed back down ***toward*** them. Sliding into the others caused a pile-up. A large snowball of sheep, gaining size as it went, tumbled back to the bottom again, landing in a heap. It was our turn to follow the *sheep*, back down the hill to begin all over.

Lesson learned by humans: sheep are idiots. Learned by sheep: Humans curse a lot.

CHAPTER 3

Trouble Maker

SHEEP BEG TO BE TAKEN care of. We are charmed by their gentle helplessness. They **need** us. (Note: If you lack that rescuer gene, get a <u>goat</u>, not a sheep.)

By far the greatest danger to a flock of sheep is dogs. Not feral or wolf-like canines, but cherished family pets allowed to run loose. Dogs are born chasers - good runners. Sheep, with their short legs and heavy coats, are no competition. They scatter. This suggests to the dog that it's a game - a deadly game for the ones being chased. Once a dog has overtaken his prey he instinctively grabs onto it. The sheep's skin is soft and tears easily. Blood is drawn, the sheep goes into shock and falls to the ground. That's that. A single dog, having attacked, can go through a flock in short order, taking down one sheep after another. Sheep herding breeds can develop a taste for lamb and become predators. We learned this lesson the hard way:

Years ago we were living next-door to a large sheep farm owned by close friends of ours. That Christmas, we got a German shepherd puppy "Willy" and took him next door for an introduction. Upon seeing the little guy Mrs. M—— cautioned him, "You're adorable. But you'd better not go after my sheep." At the time, it seemed like a strange reaction.

Two years later, Willy, now a black-and-tan beauty, had become a sweet, loyal friend. He acted as mascot for our business, spending his days at my husband's office. When not at work with the boss he was a companion and playmate for our eight-year-old daughter.

Our animals included horses, a pony and a few ducks and hens. Enamored of the flock next door, we were eager to add sheep to the mix. In addition to his other responsibilities, Willy now played protector to several Suffolk ewes. He took his duties seriously and, for several months, there was harmony in the barnyard.

One night at feeding time, I noticed a sheep down - bloodied - her shoulder ripped open. Frantically, I called the vet, then ran back to the injured ewe and cradled her head in my lap as I waited. Her breathing was shallow. What had happened? Were there wolves in Maryland? And why hadn't Willy warned us by barking?

Dr. Ross, the elderly veterinarian, was no stranger to sheep attacks. As he stitched up the patient, the dog lay between us, head on his paws, liquid brown eyes searching our faces. He seemed as distressed as I was. "Willy is upset." I said.

"Willy's **guilty**." Dr. Ross snapped. "if you care about your sheep you'll tie that dog up."

I was speechless.

For the next few weeks we were in disbelief about the dog's involvement in the crime. Nonetheless, we secured Willy to a tree in the yard (electric dog fences were a thing of the future). He was a model prisoner, but miserable. We felt badly for Willy and, gradually, we began to let our guard down.

One Saturday night, arriving home very late, we let him off his leash for a quick run before bringing him inside for the night. This time, instead of staying within sight, he disappeared into the darkness. Where was he going? "Willy COME!" we called, over and over. He ignored our shouts. Jumping into the car I drove around shouting his name, then returned home to a fitful sleep. Every hour I went back out to look for him. *Our* sheep were locked up. I thought of our neighbor's flock. I didn't want to phone and alarm them at two or three a.m. Surely he wasn't over there...

Six a.m. and still no dog. I picked up the phone.

Mrs. M———-, still groggy, answered and said she'd go outside to check. Within minutes, she rang back, sounding matter-of-fact. "Well, he's been here. Several of the ewes are down." The hours that followed are difficult to revisit.

Willy arrived home soon after that, looking glad to see us. I fell to my knees and ran a hand over his coat. He was covered in blood.

We called the vet and arranged to meet him next-door. Nothing we could say to our friends would undo the damage. (The mindset of most other farmers at the time was "shoot on sight" any predator caught killing sheep. We'd been spared that, but had to think quickly, what to do.)

What kind of a life would it be for Willy, used to running free, living in the city or kenneled for the rest of his life?" He had crossed a line - <u>twice</u>; we knew he would do it again. At that moment there was an emergency to deal with - no time to consider possibilities. And only one option, it seemed.

Heartbreaking for all of us. A tough lesson to learn.

CHAPTER 4

Triplets

For every ovine tale of disaster, there are many more occasions that lighten hearts and banish somber thoughts. Lambing is one of those times. The miracle of birth and the supreme cuteness of newborn lambs transcends description.

I recall a time at another farm in Maryland, when one of our older pregnant ewes, a Hampshire cross, was having problems. Gloria was a big girl, white with dark freckles on her nose. She had lambed successfully several times before - was a good Mum. The ram, a Southdown, was short and stocky with a massive, creamy fleece, considerably smaller than the ewe. We expected pleasant-looking, healthy lambs: white, black (or a combination) of moderate size. Gloria always produced twins, which made for a lot of fun. From the time they're born lambs are up and on the go. All legs! Before long they're leaping through the air. Twins are doubly cute.

Our sheep were bred in Autumn; the gestation period (time of conception to birth) is approximately five months. This meant that our lambs would be born in cold weather - usually February. Sheep and goats are "short day breeders" meaning that they mate in Fall. Before the days of antibiotics Winter lambs suffered less from infection and disease.

The weather was bitterly cold when Gloria was close to lambing. This time, however, the pregnancy wasn't going well. During the final month, she was listless - having trouble standing. After examining the old ewe, the vet announced that Gloria was carrying triplets and suffering from pregnancy toxemia (twin lamb disease). Her system was struggling to support them all. We increased her rations, hoping we had acted in time.

I turned to the 'sheep care' section of my bookshelf for advice. Following is a list of the causes of toxemia in pregnant ewes, suggested by various authors: multiple fetuses, fat ewes, thin ewes, small ewes, timid ewes, granny ewes, dental disease, parasitism, and lack of exercise." Swell.

Our recently-qualified young vet, concerned about the ewe's survival, suggested inducing labor. If the lambs were too immature, at least we could save the mother. Saturday morning she administered a shot to 'get things started'.

Our family had planned to go skiing for the week-end. I chose to stay home alone, to oversee Gloria's delivery. Saturday, around noon, wet snow began falling. It kept on steadily into the afternoon and evening. Sunday morning, after adding logs to the wood stove, I waded out to the barn. Mother sheep was standing, but shaky, fretting over three pristinely white babies! All were small and spindly. One by one I picked them up and carried them inside.

For the next few hours, the world stopped. Outside the snow continued its silent descent. I sat by the fire, watching the tiny three-some stretched out on a quilt, on the hearth. The wonder and fragility of life held me in its grip. The four of us were safe and warm together. The morning of all mornings. The memory of it is perfect, as if captured in amber.

Once the lambs were warm and alert it was essential to get them back to their Mum. The 'first milk' (colostrum) is a ewe's natural antibiotic. Without it, the lambs might die. Gloria was cooperative; her nursing instincts took over.

After noon the sun returned and, for the next few days, afternoon temperatures were balmy. I was relieved that the lambs seemed to be out of danger; they were gaining weight and squirming around nicely. But they were preemies - still fragile.

A week later, anxious to stay close to home, I offered to host a church committee meeting at the farm. Our deacon, Joan, mid fifties, was unmarried but motherly - an animal lover. She was excited about seeing the lambs.

Our meeting over, the committee members bundled up and trekked out to the lamb nursery. I was dismayed to see the three babies flopping around, too weak to stand. In the course of a few hours, the temperature had dropped. I picked up a lamb. It was ice cold.

Rushing the babies back inside we wrapped them up and force-fed them with warm sugar syrup. At bedtime Joan insisted on spending the night. She swaddled the tiniest lamb in a towel and took it to bed with her. I kept the other two near the radiator in my room. We had acted just in time. Our prayers had paid off.

Joan left next day with a deeper appreciation for the words of Christ: "Feed my lambs." [2]

---

[2] John 21:15 King James Bible

CHAPTER 5

Surprise

OUR INABILITY TO 'THINK LIKE a sheep' made for some funny situations. At our current farm my husband, Bill, was very supportive (if not wildly enthusiastic) when I decided to get back into raising sheep. We acquired a ewe - a huge, white marshmallow - and named her Victoria. It seemed only natural that her mate, an undersized black ram, be named Albert (Bertie, for short). Alas, their first year together resulted in no heirs for Victoria and Albert. Assuming the problem to be with the ram (the ewe had lambed before) we retired the impotent fellow and began looking elsewhere for a sire.

In November, toward the end of the breeding season, a chance conversation with a teacher-colleague, turned to the topic of farming. She told me that she owned a flock of Highland Sheep. Queen Victoria had <u>loved</u> the Scottish Highlands! This was meant to be. We hastily arranged to introduce *our* Victoria to the friend's handsome ram. We were back in business.

My experiences with lambing, years before, had involved the use of equipment little-changed from the Victorian era. Now, in the twenty-first century, we were moving with the times. We requested email updates from the breeder; our barn was outfitted with a baby monitor. (Webcams and sheep apps were still years away.)

On a blustery Saturday morning we loaded the ewe into a horse trailer. Delivered safely to the farm, Victoria was ushered unceremoniously into the Highland ram's shed. We beat a hasty retreat to avoid a threatening storm. Three feet of snow fell over that week-end and on Monday schools were closed. Tuesday morning, before students arrived, I sat down at my desk and scrolled through emails. My eyes fell on this one from my shepherdess-teacher-friend:

"Guess what??" it began. "Early this morning I went out to check on your ewe. She's okay but…..hope you're sitting down!…she's given birth."

She'd been there for only three days. Victoria's rotund shape and dense fleece had hidden her delicate condition. It took me a minute to process the situation. It seems Bertie (wherever he was) was a proud papa after all.

Meanwhile, happiest of events, Victoria had a darling, little white lamb. So unexpected. Things had happened so fast that we hadn't thought of baby names. Our tuned-in teenage daughter had the answer:

"Well, the lamb *was* a total surprise. Call her Secret. She was Victoria's Secret!"

A Victorian tale with a modern ending!

CHAPTER 6

Giveaway Goat

SOMETHING ABOUT ME SCREAMS "PUSHOVER" to family members and friends whenever a cast-off animal goes begging for a home. Here I stand, the statue of Livestock Liberty, calling in the night "Give me your poor (goat, sheep, horse) your limping, your starving, your huddled masses (of chickens, ducks, rabbits), the wretched refuse of your teeming barn. Send me these, the homeless! I lift my lamp beside the stable door." [3]

---

[3] "Give me your tired, your poor,
Your huddled masses yearning to breathe free,
The wretched refuse of your teeming shore.
Send these, the homeless, tempest-tossed to me,
I lift my lamp beside the golden door!": New Colossus, Statue of Liberty inscription

This perception may be flawed, but it reflects the thinking of my oldest daughter when she called from the racetrack one evening. "Mom, there's this old goat …belongs to one of the trainers…a mascot for the horses. Bad feet. Can't walk. Moves around the barns on her elbows [Oh, lovely]. It's pitiful. There's just something about her. Everyone adores her! She's ancient. Mum, you need this goat!"

Up to this point, I had raised sheep, steers, pigs, every kind of poultry (including quail and pheasants), horses, dogs, cats and rabbits. Somehow, I'd managed to avoid goats. Their reputation as wily and strong-willed escape artists preceded them. Besides, I prefer subjects that can be pushed around - lambs, calves, husbands…things like that.

My daughter's pleas fell on deaf ears, my response was immediate: "N-O! No way. Never!" But this young lady, blood of my blood, was relentless. It was September - plenty of time to work me over before cold weather came. She went to ground prepared to wait it out, with this cruel but, by now familiar, parting shot. "If you don't take her, they're going to put her down."

In October two of my sisters came to stay and we planned to go to the horse races at Laurel. My daughter and her husband were coming down from New jersey with several horses that were running that day. The sun shone in the sky, a slight breeze blew and Octoberfest Ales were on tap at the Budweiser tent. We basked in the glow of all three. The sisters enjoyed being with my daughter, the niece they hadn't seen in years.

Following the races the aunties were invited to the stables to meet the horses. The intake of cider and ale had us feeling relaxed and happy. One by one the examples of horseflesh were paraded by us. Finally (had she saved the best for last?) my daughter disappeared down the aisle and reemerged with a sickly, bag-o-bones, black and white, spotted goat gimping along on her elbows. One ear tilted forward; the other was half-missing, bitten off by a horse no doubt.

The poor thing dragged herself forward like a soldier in prone position moving through the jungle using elbows for propulsion. Her sternum bore a callous where it met the ground as did her forearms. Pathetic. Heartbreaking. Looking up, she fixed us with a weary stare. And in that moment I learned something:

Goats, when they make eye contact, convey a near-human intelligence and sensitivity. They scan your face as if trying to communicate their wisdom. One feels a kinship with the species.

Contrast this with the look in the eyes of a sheep, that says "Got food?"

My sisters and I, profoundly moved by the spectacle of Louisa, our instincts blurred by alcohol, were of one mind. We wanted to help this creature who was trying so hard to survive. Within minutes, the goat had been hoisted into the hatchback of my car ready for the trip home.

"Goats - sheep, how different are they, really?" I wondered on the drive home. "Same size and shape. They're sure to get along." And they might have, if Louisa had *known* that she was a goat. (We learned later that she'd never seen another goat, let alone a sheep.) In the barn, she hobbled past the receiving line of nosey ewes and headed out into the pasture. She looked searchingly through the fence at our neighbor's horses and, head in the air, she nickered to her new equine friends - her people. <u>Now</u> she was home with her own kind - horses!

Louisa, who had been raised on the race track, believed herself to *be* a horse - perhaps not a race horse, but still...

Over the next few months, Louisa's gaunt appearance improved and her shabby coat adopted a healthy luster. But those feet. They were horribly misshapen with overgrown hooves curling up like Persian slippers and boney spurs sprouting off in odd directions.

On the track, the maintenance of horses' feet is a top priority. The axiom 'no hoof, no horse' is particularly true in the racing world. How many times had a blacksmith and other animal lovers passed by this lame goat, ignoring the condition of her hooves? If they'd been trimmed occasionally, she could have walked upright.

We sought the help of people who knew about goats. Louisa's feet received the magic touch of our farrier and vet. The owner of the feed mill had goats; he had a go at trimming the hooves also. Together 'Team Louisa' worked to get the old girl walking.

Despite our best efforts, her knees permanently buckled forward; the muscles in her legs had withered. Nonetheless, once she *could* get on her feet, the recovery began in earnest. She always hobbled, but within a year Louisa could outrun anyone if she chose not to be caught.

One day in Autumn, Ron, our good friend and handyman, showed up to tell us about the *Blessing of the Animals* going on at our church. He was fond of this goat and suggested that, if we wanted to have Louisa included, he'd sit with her in the bed of the pick-up on the ride down. We attracted more than a few stares from motorists on the highway. This was nothing new. We'd transported sheep and other animals in our passenger cars for years.

 Arriving at the service, Louisa took her place beside two dogs, a cat and a pet rabbit. A roving reporter from the local newspaper was covering the annual event. This year, in addition to the regular cast of animal characters, the young journalist was surprised to see a lop-eared polka-dot creature grinning into his camera. Louisa made the news that week. Her picture graced the front page of the paper under the headline:

"Lame Goat - Redeemed by Love".

CHAPTER 7

Mine Mine Mine

My DAUGHTERS, TWELVE YEARS APART in age, are both animal lovers - imagine that. The youngest, Bet, having trained at the knee of her older sister, is a master at finding my soft spot. She knows I am weak - that stray animals are my Achilles heel. By the time this young lady turned ten I was putty in her hands. Now she was twenty - a seasoned pro at the animal rescue game.

We had gone several years without horses. Bet's college education had intervened. Now, back at home, she was supplementing her income by training problem ponies and exercising other people's horses. Her passion for the sport of kings had been rekindled and she wanted to have a horse of her own.

I had gone back to teaching, which left little time for taking on animal dependents. Our flock of elderly sheep had gradually died (or been pensioned off) and Louisa the goat rattled around, the sole occupant of our big barn. She sought out the company of our neighbor's horses, but it was obvious that she was lonely.

For teachers, Summer is a time of respite - of renewal. And sometimes, by August, it's a time of boredom. That August I was vulnerable, at loose ends and staring into a near-empty barn each day. When Bet told me about an aging thoroughbred brood mare who was being turned out of her lodgings I was sympathetic. Mind you, there was no mention of our adopting her. But, perhaps, I suggested, we could pay a call on the old girl - let her know that we were in her corner. 'We'll take her some carrots," I said.

It was a Thursday afternoon...

Pulling into the parking lot by the barn, we were barely out of the car before the farm manager approached us, "The owner of this animal hasn't paid her board. He's gone to North Carolina. What am I supposed to do with a twenty-year-old horse? If nobody takes her, (*Here it comes*) she'll have to be put down." I asked to see her.

Grabbing a lead shank the guy headed into the barn. While we waited Bet filled me in on the mare's history. Miney (registered name Mine Mine Mine) was a thoroughbred with excellent breeding. She had been raced in her early years and, after retirement, had produced ten foals for Bet's friend, J.B. a talented race trainer. We would look, I agreed. But we were NOT going home with this horse.

The barn manager returned leading a tall, dark, flashy mare. Unexpected. He trotted her past us and I was speechless! *A twenty year old!?* Horses of this age can be slightly sway-back or have bad teeth or feet. One that hadn't been ridden for years might be sour or mean. Miney had none of these issues. She was gentle, sweet and absolutely stunning! A dark bay color, she had delicate features, a mild, gentle eye and moved like a dream - floated on air.

The thought that this magnificent creature could be put to death was inconceivable. Bet's instincts had been spot on. She had seen something special in this mare, and I saw it too. This was a wonderful horse. And home she came.

Miney walked onto the trailer willingly and came off the same way. We led her around our yard and back to the barn. And who came out to greet her? Louisa was over the moon. Her very own horse! Here, in her barn. You could almost read the goat's thoughts, "She's all mine. Mine, Mine Mine!"

Bet had ridden Miney and knew her to be trustworthy. Instinctively, she climbed up on the fence and slid onto the horse's back: the old girl stood perfectly still, conversing with her new stable mate, Louisa.

Though she had never been jumped, the mare was eager to try. Soon she was enjoying long trail rides and the occasional horse show. As Bet says "Miney got me back into riding." Patience and expert handling brought out the best in this horse. For the next five years she enjoyed being ridden, pampered and groomed by all of us - most recently by Bet's riding students.

The heartbreak of rescuing older animals is that they are with us for so short a time. As I write this, Miney is 26 years old. She's out to pasture now with another mare who's due to foal in the New Year. I like to think that Miney communicates with the young mother-to-be assuring her that all will be well.

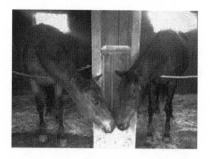

The beauty, grace and gentle manners of this
horse have been a gift to us all.

CHAPTER 8

Hand-Me-Down Dog

THE YEAR WAS 1962. SKIPPER, a well-bred Airedale terrier, was a young adult when he joined our family. My brother and I had passed by the breeder's kennel many times, always stopping to play with their dogs. This wire-haired charmer was animated, outgoing and affectionate. We campaigned hard to get him.

My parents, against their better judgement, allowed us to take ownership.

Perhaps they thought the experience would help mold their children into solid citizens. If so, they were delusional.

"This pet," they cautioned "comes with responsibility."

Soon enough we learned that, although the dog was a magnificent specimen, the breeder had spent little time on disciplining him. Our new family member obeyed basic commands - Come! Sit! and Stay - *if* he was in a responsive mood, or not distracted by the back-end of the neighbor's dachshund, Delilah.

Pre-teens when we acquired the dog, our sleeping patterns were irregular. You couldn't set the clock by any of us. And we failed to grasp the complexities of dog ownership, particularly of Airedales. They're smart but can be high maintenance, requiring lots of exercise and play. Ignore this, and you'll be looking at cavernous holes in your lawn, the result of their misdirected creative energy. And you can kiss those favorite shoes and slippers good-bye.

Skipper arrived to a triumphant welcome. Family members tripped over each other to be first at feeding him and to take him for his initial walk. The honeymoon was short-lived. Within two weeks we were drawing straws to see who got "dog duty" and by month's end the novelty of pet ownership had been stripped bare of its charm. Week-day mornings when Skipper begged to go out, we were busy grabbing breakfast and school bags. I'd fly out the door, tossing an uneaten toast crust in his direction.

Skipper, optimistic yet short on memory, was waiting to greet us when we returned home in the afternoon. Maybe *now* we'd be ready for a walk!? By then we were tired, consumed with homework or sports, or couldn't be bothered. Saturdays, the older teens went off to their part-time jobs; the youngsters preferred to sleep in or play with friends.

On the rare occasion that we *did* volunteer to take him out, we had to avoid saying the word WALK. Skipper was excitable. He'd run around madly leaving puddles on the floor. We took to spelling W-A-L-K. He was quick to decode, peeing with delight.

Skip and I had formed a bond early on, so that no one protested when I claimed ownership. In fact, the family breathed a collective sigh of relief. Now I heard:

"*Your* dog needs walking (or feeding or bathing). *Your* dog has run away, thrown up (etc.) - again! " The dog acknowledged the hand-off and shifted loyalty accordingly. He slept beside my bed, helped me with homework and ran in happy circles whenever I walked in the door.

At some point, things began looking up for old Skipper. Two things ushered in his change in luck:

The first was my Father's midlife crisis. Dad may have discovered a few grey hairs or noticed his expanding waistline. His self-image shaken, he decided to start exercising. The 5BX (basic exercise program developed by the Royal Air Force) was his regimen of choice.

Early each morning, we woke to the sound of huffing and puffing, bending and stretching. The final leg of the five-part exercise series was 'running'. It seemed only natural to head for the out- of-doors, taking the dog with him. We worried about all this physical exertion. At his office, Dad sat at a desk all day. And we feared that Skipper, badly out-of shape, might suffer a heart attack trying to keep up. However, the problem of *morning* dog-walking was solved. It remained for us to cover the evening detail.

The older siblings' entry into teen-hood was the second factor in Skipper's reversal of fortune. While our *disinterest* in the dog remained, a new *interest* in the opposite sex began to emerge.

My older brothers succumbed first; I was close behind. Suddenly, it wasn't enough that we see our love interests at school, between classes, or walk each other home. We had to phone each other an hour later - to be in communication constantly.

Our parents, fearing a neglect of schoolwork, laid down the law. <u>No telephone</u> on week-nights. Occasionally, a school event or sports practice provided a chance romantic encounter mid-week, *if* you were able to borrow the family car and take the long way home.

In today's world of social media and internet connectedness, it's hard to imagine that, in the 1960's, families had only land-line phones. These primitive devices were firmly attached to a wall, usually in a high traffic area in the home (the kitchen or front hall) within earshot of parents and siblings. We had no computers. No tablets. No cell phones. NO PRIVACY. Imagine, if you can, a time when parents were able to control a teen's communication with the outside world.

Back then there was one, and ONLY one ticket out of our house mid-week. And suddenly, walking the dog seemed like a great idea! Many of our friends lived a mile or more away; Skipper soon enjoyed long, leisurely evening walks to the park, the favorite meeting place. His dog brain must have wondered why the usual antics - jumping up and down and turning circles - were no longer necessary and why, suddenly, he was in such demand.

Poor thing. He'd limp back from these outings only to have another lovelorn sibling announce, "Think I'll take a break from homework and stretch my legs. My turn to walk the dog!" Off he'd go again - some evenings twice or three times. By this time Dad and Skip were walking several miles every morning. This was one fit canine!

Skipper remained my trusted friend until I left for University. Whenever I called home the siblings would put the receiver to his ear and I (dodging strange looks from roommates) would engage in 'dog talk' then wait for his responsive whining from the other end.

My younger sister, still at home, won him over. Skipper became hers to love and walk, and feed.

I'd handed down many things to my little sisters over the years - clothes, my old car - and now it was my dog. I passed him along with this advice: "Take care of Skipper and he'll take care of your love life!"

CHAPTER 9

Corgis

BEING OF A 'CERTAIN AGE' has its advantages. There's time to reflect on the human and animal characters who have colored our lives. Number One among my pets was a homely little dog, *Shorty*, my very first corgi. She was, quite simply, the smartest, funniest and closest-to-human dog I've ever known.

In 1985, when our paths first crossed, we were living at Stonehaven, a rambling stone farmhouse in Monkton, Maryland. We were down to one dog, an ancient Labrador retriever, and were planning to get a puppy, a smaller breed, to keep her company. Having seen and read about corgis we felt this to be the perfect choice for us. They are "big dogs in small bodies". Corgis (the name is Welsh for "dwarf dog") are bred for herding cattle. They were trained to nip at the heels of cows, yet agile enough to avoid the hooves.

"How do we *find* a corgi?" we wondered. We would compose a *want ad* to be worded as follows:

PERFECT FAMILY IN SEARCH OF PERFECT CANINE. MUST LOOK LIKE THE DOG SEEN IN PHOTOS OF THE BRITISH ROYAL FAMILY. LOVELY LITTLE RED AND WHITE, TAILLESS, CHERUBIC PUPPY. A CLASSIC CORGI.

We were spared the trouble. About that time an ad appeared in the *Baltimore Sun* newspaper:

ONE-YEAR-OLD CORGI, FEMALE. CHAMPION BLOODLINES, SIRE....DAM....CONFORMATION... TEMPERAMENT - ETC. ETC... (BREEDER TALK).

What a dog! We couldn't dial the number fast enough! We made an appointment to meet the little wonder.

On the drive over, my thoughts raced ahead to next year's Christmas card. I envisioned our perfect corgi adorned with a red satin bow, sitting by a roaring fire, the star attraction in the family photo.

Arriving at the address we knocked at the door and waited. The sound of tearing flesh and vicious snarling emanated from behind the door. A tall, frazzled-looking gentleman appeared, a homely little dog by his side. We smelled deception. Where was the bit of English finery we'd been promised? If accurate, the ad for THIS animal should have read:

MUD COLORED MUTT. STRANGE LOOKING. TOO LONG IN BODY. TOO SHORT IN LEGS. MORE EARS THAN ANIMAL. AS IS. LIQUIDATION! NO RETURNS. <u>ALL SALES FINAL</u>.

"Uhh…thank you so much." we said, upon meeting her. "She's not exactly what we had in mind. We'll see ourselves out."

The owner, an experienced dog breeder and handler, knew the quality of this animal. He could see that we were unfamiliar with the breed. While not a roly-poly *Pembroke* (the classic and familiar type of corgi), 'Shorty' was an excellent example of a *Cardigan* Welsh corgi, likely descended from Norse Vallhunds or Daschunds, which she resembled.

She and her mother, both strong females, didn't get along - they fought constantly. And corgis can be **tenacious** little scrappers.[4] Shorty's mother was the owner's best show dog. He planned to keep *her* for breeding, so this girl had to go. He insisted that she was exceptional - smart - and that she had a wonderful personality.

"So convinced am I that you will love her" he said "that I'm going to let you take her home with you. Try her out for a day." We hesitated, but, what could we say that wouldn't insult the gentleman? Off we went, the bizarre little creature in the back seat.

Once home, an amazing thing happened. Within an hour, the dog's personality had suffused our home! She'd taken over. Our Labrador was trained to stay off the sofa. This little character blew in, jumped on the couch and sat smiling as if to say, "I'm home. Now what?" We told her "Down!" She climbed

---

[4] Over the years, I've witnessed females locked in a fur-tearing, blood-drawing fight to the death. It usually happens just as visitors arrive. The dogs vie for their attention and jealousy fuels a battle. Very welcoming.

Starting the evening with a good dog fight lends a certain "edge" to a dinner party. Helps the parties work up an appetite. Before you know it, your guests have jumped in to help separate the beasts bent on dismembering each other. The trick is for you and your friends not to get *yourselves* dismembered in the process.

After this kind of old-fashioned blood sport an after-dinner game of bridge or charades will never hold their interest.

down. "Sit!" and she sat. Best of all, she loved to fetch. And... never...tired.

Her head was cocked when she listened. She made eye contact and engaged with us, asking to be part of the family. This was Shorty's most endearing quality. Some dogs are content to be left alone, others prefer the company of other dogs. This girl seemed to speak to us, to tell us what she wanted. We were charmed - ready to seal the deal.

In short order Shorty became a member of the family. I believe she would have protected us to the death.

Never having had a herding dog, Shorty's funny ways took some getting used to. With no cattle to manage, she rounded up anything she thought needed herding. In Monkton, that year, we had an abundance of vultures. They stared down from the tallest pines, like sinister, medieval gargoyles. Then, swooping from their perches, they'd circle overhead while scanning the fields below for signs of carrion.

Shorty loved this! She would take off down the hill and, looking heavenward, she'd trace the arc of their flight from the field below. Round and round the pasture she'd run, appearing to think that she, personally, had coaxed their random flight patterns into orderly formation and had hypnotized the birds into submission. Her task completed, she'd spin off and head back toward home, like a triumphant athlete.

For years, we were entertained by Shorty's daily work-out. She circled the fish pond herding frogs. She herded children. And she helped herd the chickens into the coop at night.

At that time, our business office was in the historic hotel building a short walk from home. A hiking trail led from our house to work. Shorty quickly found her way between the two places and made herself at home in both. She wanted to be where *we* were. Long after we had moved out of the offices, Shorty, a creature of habit, would walk down to the hotel and hang out with the neighboring occupant, a good friend of ours (and hers). The dog's homely appearance and sweet nature endeared her to everyone.

It was these qualities that bought her a moment of fame. My girlfriend was directing a production of "A Midsummer Night's Dream" at the high school. She needed a real dog for the play-within-a-play scene and cast Shorty in the part. As the curtains opened, there she stood, center stage - huge ears, knitted brow and confused expression, blinded by the lights and looking anxiously out into the theater - overwhelmed by the audience who howled with laughter at the sight of her. Shorty danced on her stubby little legs and was led off-stage to thunderous applause. On cue. Tail wagging.

Sticks. Shorty had to have one. In almost every photograph of the dog (and there are 15 years' worth) she has a stick in her mouth. She appears in the background of family and group photos, the signature stick protruding from her mouth like Winston Churchill's cigar. Look carefully at the shot of the family taken in the den (or living room or kitchen). There she'll be, looking in through the window. Stick in mouth.

Shorty lived for the chase. It was her way of engaging with the family. She carried a stick the way a tennis player keeps her racket close by or a golfer stores his clubs in the car. She was *at the ready*, prepared for a pick-up game whenever the mood struck her humans. For want of a stick, there'd be nothing to fetch.. Searching for one might slow things down, cut in on game time, or cause us to lose interest.

One half-expected Shorty to speak: "I <u>have</u> a stick. Let's play!" Of course had she been capable of speech, she could never have uttered those words…not with that stick in her mouth.

During family visits, my Father - the only person who could match Shorty's energy - played with the dog for hours. During their hikes on the nature trail, Dad the indulgent grandparent, collected and stock-piled sticks for their games of fetch. We were poor hosts. Boring. Shorty kept our guests entertained.

My sisters' visits were crazy times, with laughter and lots going on. Shorty was in her glory - one of the girls! I recall one of their stays, when the poor old dog was approaching senility. I overheard a sister at the back of the house announce "Shorty's asking to go out!" She opened the kitchen door. Exit Shorty. Within seconds another sister called from near the front door "The dog wants in." She let her in. This went on and on. Shorty was out.

Shorty was in. Her addled brain told her to keep moving. I now know the feeling.

Shorty was a character and that's how she'll be remembered. One day, long after I'm gone, people may draw a blank at the mention of my name. But perhaps, after careful thought, acquaintances will experience a sudden flash of recall:

"Ah yes." they'll say. "I remember Eliza! She was the one who had that little dog, Shorty."

CHAPTER 10

Farm Dog

IT WAS 1976. GOOD-BYE TO townhouse living in suburban DC. Forwarding address: Loudoun County, Virginia - the Shenandoah Valley! Overjoyed, my husband and I started gearing up for farm life.

For me, it meant one thing: <u>animals</u>. We'd need some. For starters, a proper dog. Our small, mixed-breed terrier would do as a secondary (support) animal. But, if we were going to hold our heads up - look those farmers in the eye - a larger canine breed was called for. You don't want to get off on the wrong foot with these folks, give neighbors the impression that you're "townies". We needed a farm dog.

A humble mix-breed, German Shepherd - Collie perhaps, would be the perfect choice. The intelligence of the one and the sweetness of the other make for a great all-round animal. We'd known many of these dogs on the farms of family members and friends. They tend to be low-key, vigorous and content to spend their days outside. Best of all, the puppies are usually 'free to a good home'. It made perfect sense.

But there were other considerations. Only a good-natured, lovable and high-energy dog would fit our family's lifestyle. And what about our image? Mongrels aren't bred to be beautiful.

For these reasons, we opted for a purebred Labrador Retriever. In addition to being wonderful family dogs, Labs make a strong fashion statement. The arm candy of the sporting set, they are the perfect accessory at horse races, tailgate picnics and 4th of July concerts. Add a preppy collar, one with ducks or pheasants, and you're set!

The pleasure of owning a well-bred Labrador, is that they instinctively take to water and **love** to retrieve. We located a black, nine-month-old puppy (named Puck) in need of a home. She seemed sweet enough, but we neglected to ask about her family tree or attributes. Too bad. Puck hated water. And she couldn't retrieve.

Nothing about Puck was "Puck-ish". Named for the lively sprite in Shakespeare's 'A Midsummer Night's Dream', our girl was neither lively nor spritely. What to compare her to? Not a rose, or a Summer's day. More like...a zucchini. Puck was, to the canine breed, what a zucchini is to cuisine: a blank slate. Add embellishments and condiments but the underlying thing (zucchini or dog) remains bland and unremarkable. Strictly filler. We needed a dog. Puck filled the bill.

Our imaginative daughter, Sarah, a toddler when the dog arrived, added the color and spice needed to rescue Puck from obscurity. Before long the dog was draped in colorful dress-up clothes - a tiara on her head. Puck became a circus dog. She beamed and thumped her tail in ignorant bliss.

By the age of four, Sarah had learned to read using a set of preschool vocabulary cards. With these same tools in hand she undertook the education of Puck. The dog sat benignly, as the pictures and words were flashed in front of her. There were hidden depths to this dog, visible only to our daughter.

Puck *did* share one trait with her Shakespearian namesake. She was devious. Her arrival at the farm was, at first, uneventful. She settled down under a tree and fell asleep. We tiptoed away and busied ourselves on the other side of the house. A minute later all hell broke loose! Squawking! Fluttering! We arrived on the scene and found Puck in the chicken run, grabbing and tearing at one hen after another. We were horrified and yet...this was a motivated bird dog! She'd scaled a 5 foot wire fence.

Puck moved with us to Maryland where we rented the tenant house on a large farm.

One Saturday morning, late Winter, we took a family walk in the woods. When we returned home, Puck stayed outside, then headed *back* into the woods alone - nothing unusual. She had obviously left some scent unexplored. An hour later she hadn't returned. Mid-afternoon, no Puck. We checked with our landlady who was concerned, saying that one of the neighbors sometimes set snare traps for foxes and rabbits this time of year. Now we worried. [5]

---

[5] Snares consist of a wire or cable noose, designed to trap foxes or small prey, catching them by the neck or paw.

Returning to the woods, we rambled over hundreds of acres, walking and calling for hours. Next day - the same. And the next. Then the snow came. A foot or more. We trudged through it, but finally began to lose hope. The nights had been too cold. If trapped, she'd be frozen in the snow by now. The sleet and freezing rain followed, making searching impossible. Trappers would be kept indoors too.

Often a change in everyday habits makes our losses felt. Every morning, I was used to putting table scraps in a dish by the backdoor for Puck. After her disappearance I continued the routine, hoping to lure her home. The food sat uneaten. Eventually the *neighbor's* black Lab discovered it and, for the next few days, he stopped by for breakfast. Puck had now been gone for nearly a week.

The dark, dispiriting weather reflected our mood.

One morning, standing by the kitchen sink, I felt the sun streaming in through the window bathing my face. *Warm weather. An ideal day for a trapper to get out and check his traps.* And then the thought was gone.

I gathered the kitchen scraps, as usual, and took them outside. The black Lab lay in wait. I turned to go back inside and stopped.

Did a double take. It wasn't the *neighbor's* dog. It was Puck! She struggled past me into the kitchen and collapsed. I checked her over - head to toe. She seemed all right, but one of her front paws was swollen to three times its size. Poor Puck.

The vet confirmed our fears. He'd seen dogs trapped for several days. Never a week.

"Two things saved her life", he told us. "She was overweight and survived on her body fat. Eating snow kept her hydrated." God bless the snow. But damn that trapper.

Gradually, Puck's health returned. The formerly-lackluster canine had proven herself to be a strong survivor. We loved this dog.

A year after this incident we bought our own farmhouse directly behind the tenant house. Puck settled in nicely. Still no wild bursts of intellect but she was sweet and steadfast. Our daughter continued to provide the 'personality by proxy' that Puck lacked.

"**FIRST ANNUAL DOG SHOW**" read the banner hung above our front door.

When I came upon the scene, the porch was littered with props: balls, a hula hoop, ribbons, dog treats and a can of dog food. "What's that for?" I asked. "That," Sarah said proudly "is first prize. It's the "**Coveted Kal Kan Award!**"

At times like this good friends distinguish themselves. They listen straight-faced when invited, by your child, to participate in a back-yard dog show. They drop what they're doing and attend. Best of all, best friends buy into game day frenzy and act the part of seri-ous competitor vying for first place. Our next-door neighbor Katie W—— was this kind of friend. A doctor, she was dignified-look-ing with coiffed white hair and a tweedy appearance. Katie had a great sense of humor and was a good sport. Her dog, Duchess an ancient, overweight Beagle greeted everyone with long, drawn-out howls of delight. "Ow-oooo!!" she wailed. Bone-chilling.

On Show Day, Katie and Duchess 'sat out' most of the classes. The beagle was too fat to clear the hoop in the first event and stared into space during the Obedience Class. Then came the "Individual Freestyle" in which owners and dogs showcase their area of excel-lence. Katie stepped forward and announced with deadpan delivery:

"Duchess will **NOW** perform her famous **IGNORE THE BALL TRICK!**"

With great flourish, she paraded Duchess around and placed the ball on the ground, squarely in front of the sedentary hound.

"Duchess! Fetch!" Katie commanded. Nothing. And again, "Fetch the ball…Duchess!!" No response. Duchess was now lying down. The audience went WILD! "How *does* she (not) do it?!"

Throughout the show Puck played it cool, choosing not to outshine her guests. Rather than jump through the hoop she walked *around* it to collect her treat. The ball was thrown and off she went…right past where it lay and on into the hedge. Class after class, she allowed the other competitors to shine. Her strategy paid off.

There was great celebration at The Awards Ceremony as Puck, most splendid of dogs, collected the special "Canine Humility Award".

Puck lived into her fifteenth year. Toward the end of her life, she began to get weak and disoriented. We lifted her into and out of the house several times a day, fifty pounds of dead weight. She had to be near us. In the evenings she lay directly in front of the kitchen sink. Washing dishes meant standing three feet away and leaning *over* her to work. During the day, she lay in a heap by the front door. We stubbed our feet and tripped over as we came and went. She appeared to be going deaf and blind.

While Puck lay in this sorry state, our neighbor Warren mentioned that something was getting into his trash cans. He suspected a raccoon or large dog. Our consciences were clear. Neither of our dogs was agile enough or tall enough (we also had a corgi) to pull off the heist. After several weeks of cleaning up strewn trash, Warren determined to catch the intruder in the act. He dropped by, smiling, to share the news of his discovery. It was Puck!

Warren had watched as we carried the poor, helpless dog outside. After we went indoors, he saw her rise up slowly and limp her way across the road. She hoisted her feeble frame, just high enough to grab the rim of the garbage can and pull it over. The contents spilled, she snuffled around in the mess for several minutes before heading home and pawing at our door.

She was greeted sympathetically and carried - ever so gently - back into the house to rest.

And then, it really was the end. We agonized over Puck's condition. Should we call the vet? Anyone who has experienced an animal's decline can relate to the difficulty of the decision. After a two week period in which the old Lab was semiconscious, we took her outside one afternoon to feel the sunlight. While our backs were turned Puck managed to drag herself away. Unable to find her, we suspected that she had crawled into the woods to die. We found no sign of her that night. Next morning my husband left for work, my daughter for school, both of them believing the worst.

While they were gone I checked with local veterinary hospitals, finally calling the SPCA. A dog fitting Puck's description had been found stumbling around, not far from our house. I hurried to collect her and watched as she was brought out. For the first time in months I saw - really saw - our beloved pet. The grey muzzle. The clouded, weary eyes. And I knew.

The family had already come to terms with her disappearance. I made the decision to have Puck put down, and to take her home with me. I would bury her at the farm before the family returned home.

I wasn't thinking straight.

It takes a very big hole to bury an overweight Labrador. Yet I was determined. This was a labor of love. I chose a spot at the top of the hill overlooking the river. Puck would have liked that. It was windswept - scenic. Unfortunately, the sweeping of the wind had carried the topsoil away, leaving hardpan clay.

I toiled and scraped, finally creating a hole that, in my mind's eye, appeared "big enough". With Puck at rest, in the shallow grave, I realized that, to cover her adequately, I would need to create a mountain of earth *over* the remains - a burial mound. The task completed, I gathered smooth stones and placed them in the form of a cross atop the earthworks.

When the family came home that evening, they seemed relieved to know that Puck had been found and was now at peace. We walked together to the grave, talking fondly about how we would remember her, laying by the sink or in the doorway.

Arriving at the gravesite my husband look bemused. The large mound sat smack in the middle of the path which led down to the trail. "Whenever we go for a walk we'll stub our feet on her! We'll have to step over her!" he said. He looked down at the grave.

"Aw Puck, old girl" he sighed, shaking his head. "As in life, so in death."

CHAPTER 11

Trouper

LABS ARE A TOUGH HABIT to break. The thwacking sound of the tail on the floor. The circular swipes of same tail as it clears wine glasses off the coffee table. And that good-natured welcome when you arrive home.

Puck's presence had loomed large. We missed her.

Several months later we were visiting the farm of a friend Eileen, who sheared our sheep - an amazing horse woman and breeder of

Labrador Retrievers. We were there to admire a new litter of puppies. One in particular, a lovely black male, grabbed our attention. He was outgoing and energetic. We fell hard.

Unlike Puck, this dog was extremely well bred, with a fine, handsome head. Eight weeks old when we took him home it wasn't long before he was fetching balls and sticks. And he loved the water! We named him Trouper, after the ABBA song 'Super Trouper' which played nonstop on the radio.

Indoors or out, when we were at home the new puppy was with us. He slept indoors but had a fenced kennel, close to the house, for times when we we were gone for an hour or two. He was a "people" dog, determined to be where the action was. Ours was a high-energy family, ready and able to provide the dog with constant activities. But even we needed down time occasionally. This dog <u>never</u> did.

It was the 1980's, before the days of electric dog fences. Our ten-acre farm sat on a hill, overlooking a hiking trail: beyond that was the Gunpowder River. Evenings and Saturdays, the trail teemed with exercise seekers: joggers and bikers. In warm weather the river was busy with kayaks, canoes and flotillas of 'tubers'. Trouper hiked the trail with us and swam in the river, bounding out into the current to retrieve the sticks we threw. He made friends with everyone we met. Never knew a stranger.

This was the ideal dog - perfect in every way. That is, unless he became bored and was forced to seek excitement elsewhere. Giving us 'the slip' over the hill he'd go, ready to strike up a friendship with the first person he met. We knew he'd be gone for hours. He'd follow his hiker companions, often for miles, until they reached a waiting car, leaving Trouper stranded at some parking lot miles from home.

Chasing him down on the bike did no good. By the time we noticed his absence he'd have gotten a good head start, in who-knows-what direction. We learned to wait it out, making sure that he was never without his collar and tags, our phone number on both. At the end of the day we'd listen for the phone call we knew would come, or the sound of truck tires in the driveway. Trouper was well-known to the park ranger who regularly delivered him home.

Once, when his travels took him several miles from home, Trouper fell in with a group of construction workers and hung out with them for the day sharing their lunch. Late afternoon, when the anticipated phone call came, I gave the gentleman caller our address and prepared to meet him in our driveway.

My girlfriend had stopped by to visit. She and I were outside chatting when the truck pulled up. The driver, a shirtless, blonde, superbly-tanned and well-muscled construction worker in tight, white shorts jumped out.

"Hey girls! This your dog?" I was struck dumb, unable to answer. No words came.

It fell to my girlfriend to break the silence.

"Well done, Eliza!" she said "I see you've taught Trouper to fetch!"

CHAPTER 12

Pigs

My earlier book contains the story of three little piglets, a housewarming gift from friends who wanted to give a 'tasteful' gift. The piglets promptly escaped into the night forcing us to enlist the help of perfect strangers in rounding them up. An inglorious foray into pig farming. <u>We knew nothing!</u>

Pigs, more than any other farm animals, receive a bad rap. Our preconceived notions about them is established in childhood. We learn that overeaters "pig out", obese humans are "porkers", selfish people "hog" things. Want to insult someone? Call him (or her) a swine, a pig. If your house is a mess you live in a pigsty. The descriptors smelly, filthy, disgusting, gluttonous, greedy, pushy, come to mind. Surely swine are lustful, judging by their prolific birth rate. And there you have it - the seven deadly sins rolled into one animal. (All, that is, except pride. What animal could hold its head high under the weight of these negative epithets?)

Modern research paints a different picture of pigs (*Sus domesticus*). We now know that pigs are sentient beings, on an intellectual par with some primates. Scientists Lori Marino and Christina Colvin describe the animals as "mentally and socially similar to dogs and chimpanzees." [6] Swine have excellent spatial and memory skills, are extremely sensitive and capable of feeling frustration, fear and loneliness. Had I but known.

Over the years I've raised hogs on various farms but it was a long time before I understood them.

Here's what you learn by spending time with pigs: they enjoy company, human or that of other animals. They love being spoken to - paid attention to. They sunburn easily and love the feel of a bristle brush (dipped in cool water) along their backs on a

[6] Marino, Lori; & Colvin, Christina M. (2015). Thinking Pigs: A Comparative Review of Cognition, Emotion, and Personality in Sus domesticus. International Journal of Comparative Psychology, 28.

hot day. Pigs adore a good wallow in the muck. Outdoor pen or indoor stall - they'll turn it into a mud pit. "Why wallow?" you ask. Pigs have few sweat glands; rolling in the mud helps them cool off. Provides protection from fleas and ticks. And, if you are a pig, it feels <u>so</u> good!

Pigs stink. Not surprising, given their living conditions. Mud. Excrement.

They are voracious eaters. Omnivores. In addition to commercially-prepared feed made from soy and corn, hogs will devour vegetables, leaves, insects, and meat. They 'root' as their ancestors did, using the snout to look for grubs or roots. Pigs are nest-builders; sows root to hollow out an area in which to give birth. The animals can tear up a pasture in no time. Consequently, farmers put rings through their snouts to discourage the habit.

Large, ravenous hogs are dangerous. Observe what happens when you toss a left-over turkey carcass into the sty and you will NEVER allow your toddler to get near them!

Young animals are referred to as pigs, adults as hogs. They're easy to raise, assuming you have a large, sturdy pen or tightly enclosed pasture area. Within six months they'll weigh 250 pounds, ready to butcher or send to market, which is good to know if you plan to raise them for the table.

Loudon County, Virginia during the Nineteen Seventies was a different place and time. Many of the old farm traditions, including hog butchering, were still in practice. Out along the mountain roads, small independent meat shops still operated. Most consisted of a single room with butchering facilities out back. They smelled deliciously of woodsmoke and aging meat. These places were warm, inviting hang-outs for local farmers. Rows of huge hams hung from the rafters behind the counter. I recall one shop that showcased a huge, years-old beauty, easily weighing in at fifty pounds.

Each processor had his own unique recipe for curing country hams and bacon and customers were loyal to their chosen shop. We took our pigs to a place on the Short Hill Road. The butcher cured using salt and sugar. No nitrates. Hams and sides of bacon were smoked slowly over hickory wood. Pork chops and loins, lard, scrapple and pudding (ponhaus) were ready for pick-up within a week. It took an additional three to six months before the hams were cured.

We tried our hand at drying and curing our own pork one year. The hams were hung from the rafters of the barn. During the humid weather the meat became infested with "skippers" (flies) and the meat spoiled. After that we left it to the experts.

Local farmers butchered their own hogs over Thanksgiving weekend, in a tradition that went back a hundred years and more. The sight of rising smoke from the farms was a familiar sight on butchering day. Teams of friends and family members worked at their assigned tasks, assembly-line style. A member of the Virts family (Lovettsville, Virginia) recorded the experience:

"November was the time for butchering hogs. It has been a fall tradition in the Virts family for well over 100 years. The Raymond E. Virts family on the Long Lane in Lovettsville, Virginia always butchered on Thanksgiving day. You might consider the butchering day as a family reunion held several times each November as this even would bring together siblings, cousins and friends. There was always a friendly competition amongst Raymond's brothers to see who had the largest hog. It was not uncommon to have a hog have a dressed weight of over 400 pounds. Such a hog would produce over 40 pound hams that would be sugar cured. Most local families had a butchering and would usually slaughter form 2 - 14 hogs, depending on the size of the family.

Butchering is nearly extinct today. You will only find a hand full of families that still carry on the tradition. Hardly anyone even knows how to do it anymore. I would have to say it is a dying art." [7]

Garrison Keillor, the American author and storyteller, describes the slaughter of hogs as a ritual undertaken with reverence. Temple Grandin, animal behaviorist and advisor to the meat-packing industry, concurs.

"If we lose respect for animals, we also lose respect for our-selves. It's as simple as that. People who live close to nature experience both the cycle of birth and death. Modern people have lost this experience. Garrison Keillor's "Hog Slaughter" is a vivid recounting not of death, but of respect for life, and for that I believe it's an important story for our industry." [8]

As a teacher I had often read *Charlotte's Web*, the story of a dear little pig, to my students. Its author E.B White based the story on a real animal on his farm in Maine. In 'A Letter from E.B. White' he says:

---

[7]   http://www.virtsfamilies.com/showalbum.php

[8]   A "Hog Slaughter" commentary - by Temple Grandin - Meat and Poultry, August, 1989

"As for Charlotte's Web, I like animals and my barn is a very pleasant place to be, at all hours. One day when I was on my way to feed the pig, I began feeling sorry for the pig because, like most pigs, he was doomed to die. This made me sad. So I started thinking of ways to save a pig's life. I had been watching a big grey spider at her work and was impressed by how clever she was at weaving. Gradually I worked the spider into the story that you know, a story of friendship and salvation on a farm." [9]

I share Mr. White's affinity for the animals. My children adored our pigs, named them all and considered them as near-pets. Still, as with all animals raised for meat, the time comes to explain a hog's sudden disappearance. Like Charlotte the Spider, real life parents sometimes weave intricate webs of deceit and spin stories aimed at protecting the innocent. If we cannot save the pig, we can, at least, save our children and ourselves from the truth.

My fabrications typically began: "Mr. Pig, (Sheep, Cow) has gone to the farm of a friendly farmer who was lonely." Or this: "He's gone back to where he came from. He was just visiting." Kids may not buy it, but they play along. They can see that, like them, we are struggling.

---

[9]   http://www.harpercollinschildrens.com/HarperChildrens/Kids/AuthorsAnd Illustrators/AuthorNote.aspx?CId=10499

Two year old Sarah had the 'disappearance thing' all figured out. Her Dad disappeared onto the commuter train each morning. "Where did he go?" she would ask anxiously. She got her answer when the two of us took a later train to Washington one day, to join him for lunch. We met up in the park near his office where we fed the pigeons before going to the restaurant. After that Sarah waved her Dad off in the mornings more cheerfully, calling out for all to hear "Daddy's going to feed the pigeons!"

Sarah had learned to rationalize what she could not understand, so that, when the time came for our pig, Hamlet, to go to market, his absence was easier for her to accept. Seeing that I was struggling, Sarah played the role of adult, explaining the situation gently:

"Don't be sad, Mommy." she said "Hamlet's gone to feed the pigeons."

"You're right." I lied.

Although I could not do it today, I am grateful to farmers and country folk who raise pigs in natural surroundings - roomy pens or fenced pastures. Done well, it provides humane conditions for the animals and guarantees a food source free of unwanted additives (growth hormones and antibiotics).

The alternative, a factory system in which millions of hogs live over-crowded, stressful lives is an injustice to these remarkable creatures.

CHAPTER 13

Cats

I AM NOT A 'CAT person', in the conventional sense of the term. Felines have deigned to grace me with their presence over the years, but I have not totally succumbed - never been won over, body and soul - as true cat lovers are. Felines are amusing, their agility, hunting instincts, and coyness endearing. Yet true cat lovers feel a deep kinship with these cool creatures - a spiritual connectedness that is lost on me.

If I *were* a true cat person I'd remember every pet or barn cat we'd ever had, be able to share moving stories of their endearing traits. I'd tell you how they changed my life. I'd have cat magnets, cushions, t-shirts.

For me, trace memories of each pet remain. Nonetheless, lessons were learned from cats, and stages of my life closely associated with each.

—6—

Midnight, an aging, black, stray kitty, came first. I was six years old and, after considerable wrangling, my parents allowed me to bring him home. He slept on my bed for the next five years. What I remember most is his tragic end.

When old age overtook him, he became disoriented and incontinent. My parents, perhaps wanting to protect me from the truth (or to protect *themselves* from my histrionics) had him put to sleep while I was at school. Denied the chance to say good-bye to my pet, I cried for days. This was my first profound loss. I recall feeling powerlessness - unable to protect the animal I loved.

The incident revealed two truths, a one-two punch, difficult for a child to accept: things we love die. And parents are not infallible.

In time, we come to accept the first. Coming to terms with the second can take a lifetime.

—❧

Pets held no appeal for me in my college and young-adult years. Not for me the label of undesirable roommate who 'came with a cat' or the renter who flaunted the rules by keeping a litter box tucked out of sight. (As if *that* odor could go undetected!) Only after marriage did the acquisition of dogs and cats seem necessary - that nesting experiment, perhaps.

The next cat was Tom, a yellow barn cat who worked to keep the mice down at our first farm in Canada. It's true what they say. "Yellow cats have attitude." Tom was a no-nonsense, take-us-or-leave-us kind of guy. He never wandered and could be left for days with only food and water. Perhaps he raised an eyebrow ever-so slightly when we returned. I doubt it.

The cat's coat was thick and lustrous. During the snowy Canadian winters he was happiest outdoors or in the barn. Thanks to Tom, I've always loved a yellow cat, have had five or six of them over the years and never been bored or disappointed. Characters, every one! Tom remained at the farm when we left, to set the new owners straight.

Siamese cats came slinking and yowling into our lives in 1974. The first of these was the handsome Canuck, whom we adopted as we left Canada to live in the Carolinas. With slate-blue 'points' (face, tail and feet) and aqua-marine eyes, 'Blue Points' are the home-bodies of the Siamese breed. The cat was mild-mannered, uncomplicated and loving. Canuck moved with us from house to house (to house), along with our favorite pieces of furniture.

The grand piano I had purchased in Canada, my pride and joy, graced our living room in Charlotte, North Carolina. I played it often and, with lid fully opened, the sound resonated throughout the house. Canuck enjoyed the piano too. He lay on the bench or reached his paw up to stroke the keys as I played. Occasionally a discordant melody in the living room signaled that the cat was taking a stroll along the keyboard. Throughout his good, long life Canuck kept us entertained.

When old age finally overtook him, the cat's mind went first and then his bowel and bladder control. Poor Canuck began having accidents. He chose out-of-the-way places to relieve himself, attempting to hide the evidence. We'd find a mess by the front door, another in the clothes hamper. The smell of cat urine struck you as you walked into the house. Yet we ignored these signs that his quality of life was fading.

One sunny afternoon as I sat down to play the piano I noticed a dreadful smell closeby. I followed my nose, then regretted it. In his confused state, Canuck had jumped up into the back of the grand piano. A runny mess covered the top set of finely-wound strings and drizzled down through the others. A thick puddle of cat poo, already drying in place, lay on the instrument's delicate sound board.

I found the cat cringing behind the sofa nearby. Canuck had been such a clean kitty in his youth, washing himself regularly and never missing his litter box. Now he was reduced to **this.** He hated himself for these misdemeanors. And, in that moment, I hated him too.

Like many people I feel conflicted about the Death With Dignity Act for humans, which gives terminally ill patients a voice in ending their life.

But the incident of the cat and the piano cemented my resolve where animals are concerned. Once a cat or dog becomes confused, blind, unable to control bodily functions, and may be in pain, we need to act on their behalf. It isn't fair to hold on to them for our own selfish reasons. Where is the dignity for them? Pets rely on us to make the tough decision for them.

Canuck's end came shortly after all this happened. It was time.

CHAPTER 14

Honorable Mention Cats

'SING' A GLAMOROUS BURMESE (GLOSSY brown/black) was with us from Washington through our time in Loudoun County, Virginia. Our farmhouse sat close to the road; we worried about the cat's safety. But he was a clever boy, discovering a culvert pipe which ran under the highway. For the three years we lived there, Sing traveled back and forth through his tunnel every night to hunt both sides of the busy road.

In Maryland it was 'Iffy'. On the final day of Pony Club Summer Camp, a barrow load of cats was wheeled out of the barn. The stable manager hoped that each camper might leave with one at pick-up time. Parents were greeted by grubby, over-tired children, all of them whining for permission to take a kitty home.

We agreed to take the one least-likely-to-be-chosen, a skinny (and very pregnant) tortoise shell.

Its eyes were crusty, nasal passages clogged and the overall appearance was pretty gruesome. Her chances of survival seemed "iffy". We would do what we could.

Sadly, the cat died but not before giving birth to (and hiding) two kittens. We searched everywhere, finally discovering them wedged between two hay bales in the loft of the barn. Of the two, Ginger and Pickles, only Ginger responded to hand feeding and survived.

However… Ginger Kitty, a spirited little tortoise-shell, lived for eighteen years. She'd jump from behind a bush to scare us or pounce on beams of light in the driveway. An amazing huntress, she kept our rodent population well under control during her lifetime.

Who could have predicted that a pathetic little wheelbarrow kitty could produce such a fine cat? Ginger brought us great joy and endless hours of amusement.

To this day, as I leave the house to run errands, my husband calls after me "Don't come back with an animal!" I've gone for a dentist appointment and returned home with a kitten: a litter was discovered under the doctor's porch. I've taken children trick-or-treating and returned with baby bunnies.

A visit to our friend Sonny's farm for a load of hay is always fraught with temptation: barn cats, free for the catching! Several years ago, with my daughter and her cousin along for the ride, a wild-eyed, feral, yellow kitten joined us for the trip home. By the time we pulled into our driveway the little beast, now named Otis, was tame.

He'd obviously had a rough start in life and, once home, made it quite clear that he was done with barns and with other cats. Rather than settling in with our critters, he headed to the neighbor's field to visit with their sheep. As an adult he became part of the flock, returning home for meals, then heading back to his adopted family. Our neighbors, Janie and Parker, the flock's owners, became accustomed to seeing the sheep, sheep, sheep, sheep …. CAT grazing and lazing contentedly in the field. One could almost forget the animals weren't related, were it not for a slight lack of family resemblance on the part of Otis.

Bet's Nanny and her husband Jack, now in their eighties, were always good for a barn cat whenever our supply ran low. Jack is a sweet and gentle man. His large, yellow bank-barn sits close to a country road. For this reason the feline population is always in flux. Passing strays, lured by the supply of cat food, wander in and stay. Tomcats follow their inclinations and leave. Every now and then a passing motorist drops off an unwanted animal. With all the kitty coming and going the gene pool is a healthy one. It's unlikely that you'll find a simple-minded, six-toed cat around Jack's place!

CATS FROM THE NANNY AND JACK FELINE COLLECTION

Grey Poupon, a steely grey skulker. Not much to tell since he hid a lot, preferring to roost in high places, out of sight. Closet shelves - the barn loft. We think he had a screw loose.

Miss Marble, a tortoise shell female - a sweet, timid girl gave birth to:

McGoo and Piscataway, two yellow brothers who chose to remain at Stonehaven Farm when we moved across the road. We loved these cats. The feeling was mutual, but, try as we might we could not lure them to our new place. The first day after the move, they stood by the road meowing for us to "come back home". And that is how we learned that you can't tell a cat where to live. They decide. Stonehaven's new owner, Sarah, generously took two set-in-their-ways barn cats under her wing. We retained visitation rights.

CHAPTER 15

Cinco

AT PRESENT, WE HAVE ONE, solitary barn cat and that's the way she likes it. Before she came to us, 'Cinco', a pretty white kitty with five black spots, had been an inside cat, though you would never know it. A superb huntress, she roams the fields and woods and visits the surrounding farms.

Her former owner, Helen, also had another cat, and Cinco wasn't pleased with this 'affection-sharing' arrangement. Not enough love to go around. She signaled her displeasure, as cats will do, by marking her territory. Unfortunately, Cinco's territory was Helen's lovely home and furniture.

We had no cats at the time, and didn't offer to take this one. Too much can go wrong if a cat isn't used to being outdoors and doesn't 'know the ropes'. Instead, we suggested sending Cinco to live in Jack's barn. Helen and I dropped the cat off and left her with a blanket and a good supply of food. We were optimistic.

Two days later we got a call from Jack. The cat was gone. Not wanting to tell Helen, my husband and I determined to find Cinco. We searched Jack's barn; we stuffed printed fliers in area mailboxes and tacked them to phone poles. Then, late at night, I opened my laptop to search for images of Lost and Found white cats with black markings. There were hundreds! I stared at photo after photo until every cat looked the same to me, black splotches swimming before my eyes.

(Two hours of this and I understood why the Rorschach Test, in which subjects are asked to interpret black-on-white patterns, effectively reveals madness. I was ready to have myself committed!)

Naturally, the next morning Jack called to say that the cat had reappeared. We drove up to get her, fished her down from her hiding place in the rafters and took her home with us. We weren't taking any more chances. All this drama served a purpose. After worrying about Cinco and working so hard to find her, we were invested in this girl. We <u>did</u> want a cat, after all. Not any dime-a dozen black and white spotted cat, indistinguishable from hundreds of others. Just this one.

Cinco spent that Autumn in our barn locked safely in the feed room to keep her from escaping or running away. At Christmas, our son and his family came to stay. Our granddaughter spent the morning in the barn, showering Cinco with affection and gradually introducing her to the out of doors. From then on, the cat was content to come and go, hunting at night and returning to her chair in the feed room to sleep during the day.

For the past few years Cinco has communed with the sheep, goats and horses in our life and has entertained countless children and family members. She is, bar none, the best mouser we've ever had. She also hunts baby bunnies, chipmunks and (sadly) songbirds.

In the absence of our children and grandchildren Cinco is forced to entertain herself these days. It's clear she's bored, at times.

Recently we found a cache of birds, newly slain, in the loft of the barn. Neatly sorted and color-coded. A pile of blue ones here. Red ones over there. Cinco's version of solitaire, perhaps.

My current husband, Bill, came to me bearing a male dowry: cats.

Lizzy and Pearl, Siamese mother and daughter, were cherished members of his family before our marriage. Afterwards, Bill and I had to decide where to set up housekeeping (his house in White Hall or my place in Monkton). It was difficult enough deciding where we humans would live. What about his cats? Initially they remained at Bill's farm. We spent week-ends there and week-days at my place. It was a crazy set-up.

We gave up trying to load his cats into their crates for travel to Monkton. When we *could* catch them, they hissed and carried on until we gave up and left them behind. Every evening during the week one of us would drive the ten minutes up to feed the cats. Initially, Lizzy was aloof and hid from us. Her routine had been disrupted. She was NOT happy about it. Pearl? No problem. If it was food time, she was there. Front and center!

For Bill and me, the lines between 'his' place and mine gradually blurred. If Bill was at his farm, a fire going and a meal on the stove, it felt like home. Suddenly my place felt colder and less-welcoming. Likewise, if the meal, the fire etc. was happening at the Monkton house, we all felt at home there. The structure - the house - became immaterial.

After a time, the cats came to the same conclusion. One evening, a few weeks into our weekly housing-commute, I went to White Hall to feed 'the girls', as usual. This time, Lizzy crawled out of her hiding place to acknowledge the hand that fed her. I stayed for a few minutes, then turned to go. As I walked to my car Lizzy followed me and then, VOLUNTARILY, she climbed into her cat carrier, which was sitting by the driveway. Her message was clear. "Take me with you. Take me home."

CHAPTER 16

Alistair

IT WAS THE 1980's. MANY of us, parents of young girls, were
caught up in the doll house craze, spending small fortunes on
wooden kits and furnishings for our children's Victorian model
homes. Saturday mornings we'd be at 'Favorite Things' a shop in
nearby Hereford, Maryland housed in a cozy, pale pink, Victorian
house with moss green shutters and gingerbread trim.

The place itself resembled a charming doll's house: glass cabinets
packed full of miniature antique furnishings, lighting kits, ele-
gantly-clothed family members, hardware and household goods.
And there were gift items! The heady scents of English teas,

soaps and rose petal-and-lavender potpourri infused the place. A winding, wooden staircase led to an upstairs room where fully-assembled and painted model homes were on display. Turreted Queen Anne styles and manor houses with elegant, mansard roofs shared space with simple Gothic structures. There was even a log cabin.

When we finally decided to purchase a kit, we chose a basic Folk Victorian style, insisting that we liked its simple lines. What we *liked* was its simple assembly instructions! The completed dollhouse was placed, on a bedside table, in our daughter's room.

There it became the week-end playground for her pet mouse, Alistair.

Alistair's fur was white, his eyes pink. In the dollhouse, he loved to run up and down the tiny stairs never disturbing the furnishings nor trying to taste the realistic-looking, ceramic food items (pies and cakes) on the small kitchen sideboard. The dollhouse father, in his velvet suit, spats and starched white collar stood next to his corsetted wife, sternly disapproving of Alistair's breezing through their home. Over and under the beds the mouse ran. When exhausted the little guy would fall asleep upstairs in the miniature claw-foot bathtub.

It was clear, to us, that Alistair preferred the gilded decor of *this* house to his own, which was really a bird cage, hung from a stand near the window and lined with pine shavings.

One night I was woken from a deep sleep by our (then) six year old's screams. She had heard scuffling noises coming from Alistair's cage and jumped up to check on her pet. She freaked out when she found not one, but TWO mice in the cage. The intruder was a little grey field mouse who had managed to squeeze through the bars, attracted by the aroma of mouse food. Lifted by the tail, this country cousin was returned to the cold outdoors from whence he came and peace was restored to our home.

Some time later Sarah's teacher shared with us a story that our child had written about the incident. The tale's main character was a bon vivant - a mouse named Alistair - who threw lavish parties after lights out. He wore a white dinner jacket and strutted around addressing everyone as "Old Sport".

While amused by the story we were secretly relieved that, unlike his story counterpart, *our* little mouse was possessed of a more humble nature. Alistair had seen fit to share his meal with a less fortunate stranger.

CHAPTER 17

Hen Party

AFTER FORTY YEARS OF RAISING chickens, I remain fascinated by the elaborate dance of power - the 'pecking order'. Watching a hen join an established flock puts one in mind of human group dynamics or a scramble up the corporate ladder. The newcomer ranks lowest, pecks last and gets pecked on. She's the wallflower at the hen party.

Now watch this same, pitiful victim when another new bird comes onboard. Our benign heroine turns aggressor. Empathy? There is none. She will render her mates featherless, bloodied, and scalped. What begins as a one-on-one skirmish attracts others into the fray. Removal of the victim is the only solution.

Dottie, a black and white speckled hen (a Spotted Hamburg) was the latest addition to our current flock; she quickly fell prey to the others - didn't even put up a fight. In time, the top of her head was bald and bloody from her injuries. We removed her to a stall in the barn and set up a small wooden ladder as a perch. The corner feed bin, filled with hay, made an adequate nest. She was safe but traumatized. The poor girl stopped laying, lost interest in eating and spent her days hanging listlessly from the perch.

Eloise, our sweet yellow Nubian goat lived in the stall next door. Like Dottie, she was alone - missing her companion, our horse, who had moved to another farm for the Summer. Eloise was a survivor herself. She loved to stay close to her equine pal and one day, the horse accidentally stepped on her, breaking the goat's leg. The vet had fashioned a cast for her to wear for several weeks, but, despite our efforts, Eloise never recovered the use of the leg. She hobbled around on the other three. (What is it about us and lame goats?)

We wondered if the chicken and goat might find comfort in being together, and opened the door to the chicken's stall. After a few minutes, Eloise wandered in to check things out. (and also to look for food). She bedded down below the hen and, within hours, the two of them were eating from the same bowl. No bullying. They kept each other company all Summer and, when the horse returned in the Fall the old friendship of goat and mare expanded to include Dottie the hen.

Soon after the mare's return I slipped out to the barn one night, catching the friends unaware. The horse was standing quietly with Eloise, the goat lying nearby; the speckled hen was roosting - nodding off - perched on the horse's back. An unlikely friendship born of a hen's misfortune. Shakespeare observed that "misery acquaints a man with strange bedfellows".[10] Strange indeed.

On the subject of egg laying, we've learned a few things over the years:

Hens lay more prolifically when a light source is provided: their brain's pineal gland signals the release of hormones resulting in egg production. In Autumn and Winter when the days are short laying 'falls off'. Want more eggs for Winter breakfast? Provide artificial light in the coop.

---

[10] *The Tempest* (2.2)

Hens lay a fixed number of eggs in their lifetime, the total depending on the breed. Chickens who no longer lay, or who lay sporadically, are 'spent' hens. What to do with them then is a matter for the farmer to decide: keep them on as pets, give them away or put them in the stew pot. In my experience, the last choice is the least appealing. Plucking and processing chickens is messy work, the meat from old hens often tough and stringy. (My opinion.) I've always had good luck finding homes for mine, as there's always someone who seems eager to "have a few hens around" whether or not they lay. To those souls I say a heart felt "Thank you!" while secretly thinking "You're nuts."

Some hens are broody; they have the urge to sit on eggs and hatch them. Many of today's hybrid hens, purchased from large suppliers, have had the broodiness 'bred out' of them, with egg production taking precedence over hatching chicks. Bantams love sitting on eggs and are great mothers. They'll eagerly hatch chicks any time of year. At this writing, two of my banties have a brood. It's October and cold, but the hens keep their babies warmly tucked 'up under' where the temperature is a cozy 100 degrees! (as registered by our kitchen thermometer).

More and more people are discovering the joy of raising backyard poultry. They are easy to keep, fun to watch and <u>nothing</u> compares to those really fresh eggs! However, be forewarned: chickens are endlessly amusing - great time wasters. Expect to spend hours watching them scratch and peck. You'll worry about their loss of feathers or lack of appetite. A friend of mine sews protective clothing for her girls! And, when you tell people who don't have animals, how you spend your time, just don't be surprised if they look a bit concerned…about *you.*

CHAPTER 18

Olga the Guinea Pig

HERE IS A SIMPLE STORY that illustrates the resilience of children.

Olga was our five-year-old daughter, Sarah's, pet guinea pig. She had deeply-swirled white-and-tan fur and an expression of sweet contentment on her face. Every day, after school Sarah took her pet from its cage and the two of them read or watched TV, Olga nestled in her mistress' lap. We had little contact with the animal. Our presence was not required.

The guinea pig's cage life was uneventful. Feeding time provided her major entertainment. Olga created intrigue for herself by burying her pellets under the shavings, then rooting around to 'find' them. We decided to spice up her routine by switching to a pricier brand of guinea pig food. Maybe a new flavor and larger-sized pellets would help break the monotony for Olga.

A week later, as Sarah was putting her furry friend back in its cage she remarked that Olga was "wobbly". I picked up the little guinea pig and noticed immediately that she was skin and bones. I tried setting her down. She couldn't stand. Checking her cage I saw the problem. She hadn't touched the new pellets, all of which were buried in her shavings. The guinea pig hadn't eaten for a week! I was overcome with guilt.

Reading the expression on my face Sarah asked sadly "Is Olga going to die?'

A short time later, when her Father came home, Sarah, now in tears, asked him the same question: "Is Olga going to die?"

The skeletal little pig lay bundled up in Sarah's lap as we drove to the vet's office. The doctor was waiting for us, the door to his examining room open. He placed Olga on the stainless steel table. Her legs immediately gave out. She flopped around uncontrollably.

Looking over our daughter's blond curls the vet's eyes met ours. He shook his head back and forth to signal, to us, the futility of the situation. We were overcome. How would we break the news to Sarah? Could she survive the loss of this dear, little pet? We looked at each other helplessly.

A small voice broke the gloomy silence:

"If Olga dies," Sarah chirped "Can I get a brown one?"

I reflect on my parents handling of my cat Midnight's death all those years ago and of the many times since then that we have sheltered our own children from such harsh truths. If Olga's story taught me anything, it's that children need to be included in life and death decisions regarding animals. Believe me, they're stronger than you think.

CHAPTER 19

Hedgehogs

WHY NOT START A PRESCHOOL? It was 1993 and the vestry of our small country church had been discussing three areas of concern: improved community outreach, attracting young families to the parish and financing the upkeep and repairs on the 100-year-old buildings. I suggested that a church preschool might help with all three, and volunteered to spearhead the project.

It was exciting to think what kind of school it would be. The church's setting was idyllic, surrounded by woods and open farm fields. Children could explore nature and learn skills hands on. The emphasis - learning through play. No TV and no computers. Animals? Always welcome!

During my time at the preschool, we handled spiders, toads, insects, and frogs. The dedicated and gifted teachers welcomed visiting lambs and ducks. Together we observed the magic transformation of caterpillars to Monarch butterflies.

Our preschool logo, a little hedgehog, was inspired by Mrs. Tiggy-Winkle a character created by Beatrix Potter, author of *Peter Rabbit*. As luck would have it, pet stores began selling pygmy hedgehogs about that time. I had to have one! He'd be the perfect school mascot.

'Hedgie' came to the preschool every day and charmed his way into our daily routine. That same year we discovered the books of Jan Brett. Her hedgehog (also named Hedgie) and the amazing illustrations delighted our students and teachers. We eagerly awaited each new book as it was published.

A hedgehog is a wonderful pet for young children. Ours became very tame. Preschoolers learn quickly that rough handling and sudden movements cause the small animal to roll into a prickly ball. The spines hurt! Instinctively, students calm down and lower their voices.

The hedgehogs - we had several over the years - had their own adventures. At times, we allowed them free run of the schoolroom. But these little critters move quickly. Every now and then we'd have to mount a 'Hedgie hunt'.

Once, at the end of the day, the hedgehog was still missing. Knowing that the animals are nocturnal. I decided to come back in the evening to look for him, expecting to find Hedgie running around in plain sight. Unfortunately, the heat had been turned off to save on fuel.

Hedgehogs, if they get too cold, go into a state of hibernation, curling up and staying put. I didn't find him that night or for two more nights. Evening three I was beginning to worry that our little pal might starve to death. I finally discovered his hiding place; he was rolled up tightly under the water cooler. Great relief! I had been dreading the 'teachable moment' ...."Do hedgehogs go to heaven?"

The Preschool had been in operation for less than two years when my first husband Jay died unexpectedly. It was necessary for me to take a leave of absence. It was a difficult time for my two daughters. The oldest, Sarah, returned to college shortly after losing her Dad. The University arranged for her to have a private dorm room. She asked if she could take Hedgie with her, for company.

As Mother and daughter we worried about each other. Talking about our loss was overwhelmingly difficult; the pain too fresh. In typical Sarah fashion, she conveyed her support in a light-hearted way, by having the hedgehog write me a note from college.

Here's a picture of the little guy, now a cool college dude, looking a bit 'wasted'.

Hedgie wrote:

> *"Hello Mum*
> *How's it goin' ? I have found my niche right here in the middle of the swingin', fast-paced social scene at St. Johns. It takes spines to keep up with the tough crowd I'm in with, an' I got 'em man. I tell you, they don't call me Spiny Norman for nothin' - Spiny the Leisure Ninja, that is, rockin' this scene like no other*

***Euro-rodent can. Hang in there hon! I'll be makin' my
way back home soon, when the fun's over here -
Stay cool,   Your "Hedgie"***

For the first time in weeks, I laughed out loud. I knew my daughter would be OK.

I wasn't so sure about Hedgie.

—❦

Back at home, Hedgie loved to run around in the grass and he was fast! Look away for a few seconds and he'd be hiding under a bush or in the garden.

A day in Springtime, several years later comes to mind. I was remarried to a wonderful guy, Bill. As loving couples sometimes do, we had argued and exchanged harsh words. He, no doubt, was in the wrong. We weren't speaking. He had tried to patch things up; I wasn't having it. Wouldn't budge.

Mid-afternoon we heard the kids on the street calling for the hedgehog. He was lost, <u>again</u>. Already cross from arguing, I became anxious and distressed. *What if Hedgie is gone, for good, this time?* It was late afternoon. The sun was setting and no sign of him. My husband, still trying to get on my good side, dropped what he was doing and joined in the search. We looked over and under rocks, around shrubs and in the deep grass.

Just when I had given up hope of finding our precious pet, Bill's voice rang out from the other side of the house. Loud and clear. I rounded the corner...there was my husband, on his knees, holding the hedgehog up towards heaven.

"RE - DEMP - TION!!" he shouted.

Hedgie was found. All was forgiven.

Bill and I are entering life's 'quiet zone'. The number of animal friends in our menagerie has dwindled: two dogs, a barn cat and a few hens - a poor showing by past standards. My lovely old mare died recently leaving a hole in my heart big enough to drive a tractor through.

A recent convert to social media, I received two messages last week from friends who remembered my love of hedgehogs. I took it as a sign. Large barn animals may be in my past, but a little hedgie - perhaps one who needs me? I went window shopping online ...

Enter Bella. This little rescue-case arrived in a filthy cage, her food rotting under sodden shavings. The hedgehog, resembling a prickly pear, had rarely seen the light of day. Because of her tendency to roll into a spiny ball when first picked up, the former owners thought she was asking to stay put. If only they had known that, with regular handling, these pets can become tame and animated little family members. Bella hissed when we approached. The owners left her with us, saying, "She's really unhappy and not friendly. Forget trying to touch her. She doesn't like people!" That was then.

Bella has a new evening routine. At exactly eight p.m. she climbs over the sofa cushions and chows down on finely-chopped leftovers (pate is her favorite). Dinner digested, she crawls along for a few feet and looks for Bill. Bella steps confidently off the couch and onto his outstretched hands, drops into his lap and, using him as a human escalator, she climbs down his outstretched legs and onto the floor. Off she goes for her evening scamper around the house.

Bella's transformation has us feeling proud. But this is not the way we imagined spending our golden years!

These days, our animal family is a small one. My dear old barn, once a hub of activity, stands empty. But animal lovers are a rare breed. For us, the final chapter is always…..yet to be written.

Animals

"They are not brethren, they are not underlings; they are other nations, caught with ourselves in the net of life and time, fellow prisoners of the splendor and travail of the earth." **– Henry Beston**

About the Author

ELIZA RUSK LIVES ON A farm in Maryland with her husband Bill, 2 corgis, Cinco the cat, Bella the hedgehog and assorted hens.

Animal Stories is Book 2 in the series: 'This Country Life'.

Epilogue

⚬

THE **SHEEP MEMO** WRITTEN BY Lammott DuPont Copeland intrigued me. I wanted to know more about the Dupont family and their experiences raising sheep. The archivist at Mt. Cuba, the former Copeland family estate in Delaware, could offer no help. He knew only that cattle had been raised there - no sheep. I decided to dig deeper. My exploration uncovered these tidbits of Dupont sheep history:

- a Spanish treaty concession paid in sheep
- Don Pedro, the world-famous Merino
- Thomas Jefferson's killer ram, the "abominable animal"
- a secret Cold War testing site for chemical weapons

Want to know more? Follow these links:

https://thefiberarchive.com/2016/04/29/first-flock-merino-mania-white-house-wool/#more-1352

http://museumblog.winterthur.org/2013/06/26/the-sheep-at-negendank-barn-a-fine-wooled-history/

https://books.google.com/books?id=Us8KAQAAIAAJ&pg=RA5-PA6&lpg=RA5-PA6&dq=spanish+treaty+4000+merino+sheep&source=bl&ots=GoihX1oCHs&sig=gkwvfhFbYhPVJWaNLRjCZinPNRI&hl=en&sa=X&ved=0ahUKEwi61OKRncjRAhVD3SYKHX11C64Q6AEIHDAA#v=onepage&q=spanish%20treaty%204000%20merino%20sheep&f=false

https://www.amazon.com/Du-Pont-Dynasty-Behind-Curtain/dp/0818403527

40892726R00086

Made in the USA
Middletown, DE
26 February 2017